The Ultimate Coffee Recipe Book

101 Recipes for Lattes, Flavored Syrups, and Classic Coffee Drinks

Stella Rose Wilder

Copyright 2023 Stella Rose Wilder

All rights reserved worldwide. No part of this book may be reproduced or transmitted in any form or by any means electronic or mechanical, including photocopying, recording or by any information storage and retrieval system without written permission from Stella Rose Wilder.

Printed in the United States of America

Stella Rose Wilder. *The Ultimate Coffee Recipe Book: 101 Recipes for Lattes, Flavored Syrups, and Classic Coffee Drinks*

Cover Image: © Kartik Sharma/Wirestock Creators/ Adobe Stock https://stock.adobe.com/images/vertical-close-up-shot-of-a-beautiful-cup-of-cappuccino-with-romantic-latte-art/516362803"

Disclaimer/Warning:

This book is intended for lecture and informative purposes only. This publication is designed to provide competent and reliable information regarding the subject matter covered, although inaccuracies may be present. The author or publisher are not engaged in rendering legal, medical, or professional advice. Laws vary from state to state and if legal, financial, medical, or other expert assistance is needed, the services of a professional should be sought. The information in this book is not meant to replace professional medical or nutritional advice. The author and publisher disclaim any liability that is incurred from the use or application of the contents of this book.

"May your coffee mug always be full, your latte art Instagram-worthy, and your espresso shots stronger than your willpower to resist them."

Contents

Introduction 8
The Global Phenomenon of Coffee 8
The Romance of the Bean 9
A Symphony of Flavors 9
The Culture and Community 10
The Science Behind the Art 10

Classic Coffee Drinks 12
Espresso..13
Americano 14
Latte 15
Cappuccino 16
Macchiato 17
Breve..18
Flat White 19
Café au Lait 20
Vienna Coffee 21
Cold Brew Coffee 22
French Press Coffee 23
Turkish Coffee 24

Flavored Syrups 25
Classic Syrup 26
Vanilla Syrup 27
Hazelnut Syrup...28
Coconut Syrup..29
Lavender Syrup 30
Pumpkin Spice Syrup...31
Caramel Brulée Syrup 32
Almond Syrup 33
Coconut Syrup..34

Raspberry Syrup 35
Toffee Nut Syrup 36
Salted Caramel Syrup 37

Classic Flavored Lattes **38**
Vanilla Latte 39
Hazelnut Latte 40
Mocha Latte 41
Coconut Mocha Latte 42
White Chocolate Mocha 43
Caramel Macchiato 44
Café Miel Latte 45
Maple Latte 46
Coconut Latte 47
Matcha Latte 48
Pistachio Latte 49
Tiramisu Latte 50
Spiced Chai Latte 51

Artisanal Flavored Lattes **52**
Lavender Vanilla Latte 53
Pumpkin Cardamom Latte 54
Maple Sage Latte 55
Orange Mocha 56
Cinnamon Roll Latte 57
Spicy Mexican Mocha 58
Turmeric Ginger Latte 59
Nutella Latte 60
Brown Sugar Latte 61
Honey Latte 62
Butterscotch Latte 63
Thai Latte 64
S'mores Latte 65

Holiday Inspired Lattes 66
Pumpkin Spice Latte.. 67
Gingerbread Latte 68
Candy Cane Latte 69
Eggnog Latte 70
Holiday Spice Latte... 71
Valentine's Cardamom Rose Latte 72
Thanksgiving Apple Pie Latte 73
Christmas Peppermint Mocha..................................... 74
Cranberry Bliss Latte 75
Winter Wonderland Latte 76
Spiced Orange Latte 77
Maple Pecan Pie Latte 78
Cherry Blossom Latte 79

Iced Flavored Lattes 80
Iced Brown Sugar Oat Milk Latte 81
Iced Salted Honey Latte 82
Iced Honey Lavender Latte.. 83
Iced Dirty Chai Latte... 84
Iced Cinnamon Dolce Latte 85
Iced Toffee Nut Latte... 86
Iced Caramel Brulée Latte 87
Iced Vanilla Sweet Cream Latte 88
Iced Pumpkin Cold Brew Latte 89
Iced Honey Cinnamon Latte 90
Iced Salted Maple Cold Brew Latte............................... 91
Iced Raspberry Mocha 92

Blended Coffee Drinks 93
Classic Frappuccino.. 94
Creamy Coffee Smoothie 95

Mocha Frappuccino 96
Caramel Frappuccino 97
Java Chip Frappuccino.. 98
Coconut Milk Mocha Macchiato Frappuccino 99
White Chocolate Mocha Frappuccino 100
Strawberries And Crème Frappuccino............................... 101
Green Tea Frappuccino 102
Pumpkin Spice Frappuccino 103
Mint Mocha Frappuccino 104
Salted Caramel Mocha Frappuccino 105
Raspberry Coffee Milkshake... 106

Coffee Cocktails 107
Espresso Martini 108
Irish Coffee.. 109
Black Russian 110
White Russian 111
Kahlua Coffee.. 112
Nutty Irishman 113
Mexican Coffee with Tequila and Kahlua.......................... 114
Bourbon Spiked Hot Coffee 115
Café Amore with Amaretto and Cognac 116
Spanish Coffee 117
Coffee Old Fashioned 118
Cold Brew Negroni.. 119
Amaretto Tiramisu Coffee 120

Introduction

The Global Phenomenon of Coffee

Coffee isn't merely a beverage; it's an embodiment of numerous emotions and experiences. As you stand at the bustling counter of your favorite coffee shop, waiting for your freshly brewed cup, take a moment to realize that you are partaking in a global phenomenon. From the quaint alleyways of Vienna to the bustling streets of Istanbul, from the coffee plantations of Brazil to the artisanal coffee shops of Portland, coffee is more than a drink – it's a language that millions speak.

The Romance of the Bean

Every sip of coffee has a history, a lineage. The beans in your cup might have sprouted in the highlands of Ethiopia, bathed in the sunlight of the Costa Rican shores, or grown under the shade of trees in Sumatra. These beans have witnessed sunrises and sunsets, monsoons and droughts, before being carefully selected by diligent farmers.

Post harvesting, the beans embark on a transformative journey. The roasting process unlocks a plethora of flavors hidden within them. A good roast can highlight the bean's natural flavor, whether it's fruity, nutty, chocolaty, or floral. This is the alchemy that turns a simple seed into a source of daily delight for billions.

A Symphony of Flavors

Every coffee drinker has their preference. Some swear by the classic black, savoring every bitter note. Others prefer the comforting embrace of a creamy latte or the sweet delight of a caramel macchiato. And then there are the adventurers, always looking for the next unique blend, be it a turmeric-infused coffee or a cold brew with hints of lavender.

The beauty of coffee lies in its versatility. With just one bean as the foundation, the spectrum of flavors one can create is staggering. This book aims to introduce you to this vast and flavorful world. Every section, every recipe, is a new chapter in the vast anthology of coffee.

The Culture and Community

To understand coffee is to understand its culture. Think about the traditional Italian espresso bars, where locals stand and gulp down their shots, or the Swedish 'Fika' – a concept in Swedish culture meaning "to have coffee", often accompanied with pastries, cookies or pie.

Then, there are the modern-day coffee shops, each with its own personality. Some are buzzing hubs of networking and rapid laptop typing, while others are tranquil spots perfect for reading or reflection. These places aren't just about coffee; they're about community, connection, and camaraderie.

The Science Behind the Art

Making the perfect cup of coffee is both an art and a science. Variables like grind size, water temperature, and brew time can greatly influence the taste. The difference between a sour or a bitter cup can be a matter of seconds in brewing or a slight change in temperature.

This is why precision matters. And it's also why making coffee can be so rewarding. There's a sense of achievement in brewing that perfect cup, in understanding the nuances of what went into it, and in savoring the result of your efforts.

This book is not just a collection of recipes; it's a journey. A journey through cultures, through flavors, and through the many stories coffee has to tell. As you explore its pages, we hope you find not just the taste you're seeking, but also the stories behind them. We've curated a mix of the classics that have been beloved for decades and the innovative recipes that are redefining coffee consumption today.

So, as you brew each cup, remember: You're not just making a beverage; you're partaking in a global ritual, a shared experience, a timeless tradition. And with each sip, you're making memories, one cup at a time.

CLASSIC COFFEE DRINKS

Embark on a journey through the timeless classics of coffee culture. From the robust simplicity of espresso to the creamy allure of a cappuccino, this section celebrates the foundational drinks that have shaped our global coffee experience. Dive in and rediscover the essence of coffee.

ESPRESSO

Prep Time: 2 Min

Serving: 1

INGREDIENTS:

18 to 20 grams of finely ground coffee beans (preferably a dark roast)
1 ounce (30 milliliters) fresh, filtered water

INSTRUCTIONS:

Preheat your espresso machine. While it's warming, grind your coffee beans to a texture resembling fine sand.
Measure and dispense 18 to 20 grams of freshly ground coffee into the portafilter. Tamp down the grounds firmly and evenly with a coffee tamper.
Insert the portafilter into the espresso machine's group head. Start the shot and allow the machine to dispense approximately 1 ounce (30 ml) of espresso. This process should take about 25-30 seconds.
Serve the espresso immediately.

AMERICANO

Prep Time: 2 Min

Serving: 1

INGREDIENTS:

1 shot (1 ounce or 30 millilitres) of espresso
6 ounces (180 milliliters) hot water

INSTRUCTIONS:

Prepare a shot of espresso using the method described in the previous recipe. While preparing the espresso, heat 6 ounces of fresh, filtered water to about 200°F (93°C). In a serving mug, first, pour the hot water. Gently add the prepared shot of espresso into the mug with hot water.
Give it a good stir and serve immediately.

LATTE

Prep Time: 5 Min

Serving: 1

INGREDIENTS:

1 shot (1 ounce or 30 milliliters) espresso
8 ounces (240 milliliters) whole milk

INSTRUCTIONS:

Brew a shot of espresso. While brewing, steam the milk until it reaches a creamy, velvety consistency.
Pour the espresso into a serving mug. Gently add the steamed milk to the espresso, holding back the foam with a spoon and allowing the liquid milk to pour first.
Top with milk foam (a thin layer) and serve immediately.

CAPPUCCINO

Prep Time: 5 Min

Serving: 1

INGREDIENTS:

1 shot (1 ounce or 30 milliliters) espresso
5 ounces (150 milliliters) whole milk

INSTRUCTIONS:

Prepare a shot of espresso and pour into a cappuccino cup. Steam the milk until it has a good amount of foam—about double in volume.
Spoon the steamed milk and foam over the espresso. Aim for equal parts of espresso, steamed milk, and foam in the cup.
Serve immediately.

MACCHIATO

Prep Time: 5 Min

Serving: 1

INGREDIENTS:

1 shot (1 ounce or 30 milliliters) espresso
1-2 teaspoons (5-10 millilitres) steamed milk (dairy or plant-based)

INSTRUCTIONS:

Brew a shot of espresso into an espresso cup. Steam a small amount of milk until it's frothy. Add a dollop or spoonful of milk foam to the espresso shot.
Serve immediately.

BREVE

Prep Time: 5 Min

Serving: 1

INGREDIENTS:

1 shot (1 ounce or 30 milliliters) espresso
8 ounces (240 milliliters) half-and-half

INSTRUCTIONS:

Brew a shot of espresso. While the espresso is brewing, steam the half-and-half to a velvety consistency.
Pour the espresso into a serving mug. Add the steamed half-and-half to the espresso. Serve immediately.

FLAT WHITE

Prep Time: 5 Min

Serving: 1

INGREDIENTS:

2 shots (2 ounces or 60 milliliters) espresso
6 ounces (180 milliliters) steamed whole milk

INSTRUCTIONS:

Brew two shots of espresso into a serving cup. Steam the milk to a microfoam consistency with very tiny bubbles, ensuring it's velvety and not too frothy. Spoon the steamed milk over the espresso shots, allowing a thin layer of microfoam to top the drink. Serve immediately.

CAFÉ AU LAIT

Prep Time: 5 Min

Serving: 1

INGREDIENTS:

6 ounces (180 milliliters) of freshly brewed strong drip coffee or French press coffee
6 ounces (180 milliliters) whole milk

INSTRUCTIONS:

Brew the coffee. While coffee is brewing, heat the milk over medium heat until it's warm but not boiling. Froth the milk as per your preference.
Pour the brewed coffee into a large mug and add the warm milk. Serve immediately with your preferred sweetener and a dusting of cocoa powder if desired.

VIENNA COFFEE

Prep Time: 5 Min

Serving: 1

INGREDIENTS:

2 shots (60 milliliters) espresso
2 ounces (60 milliliters) whipped cream
chocolate shavings or cocoa powder (for garnish)

INSTRUCTIONS:

Brew two shots of espresso and pour them into a coffee mug. Top the espresso with a generous amount of whipped cream. Garnish with chocolate shavings or a dusting of cocoa powder. Serve immediately.

COLD BREW COFFEE

Prep Time: 10 Min

Serving: 2

INGREDIENTS:

1 cup (about 100 grams) coarsely ground coffee beans
4 cups (950 milliliters) cold water

INSTRUCTIONS:

Combine the coarsely ground coffee and cold water in a large jar or pitcher. Stir the mixture well to ensure all ground coffee is fully saturated.
Cover and refrigerate for at least 12 to 24 hours. After the brewing time, strain the coffee thoroughly with a fine-mesh sieve into a clean pitcher.
Serve the cold brew over ice, diluted with water or milk to taste.

FRENCH PRESS COFFEE

Prep Time: 4 Min

Serving: 2

INGREDIENTS:

1 ounce (28 grams) coarsely ground coffee
16 ounces (475 milliliters) boiling water

INSTRUCTIONS:

Add ground coffee to the French press. Pour the boiling water over the grounds, ensuring all the grounds are saturated.
Place the lid on the press with the plunger pulled up. Let the coffee steep for about 4 minutes. After steeping, slowly press down the plunger. Pour the brewed coffee into a mug and serve immediately.

TURKISH COFFEE

Prep Time: 5 Min

Serving: 1

INGREDIENTS:

1 cup (240 milliliters) cold water
1 tablespoon (7 grams) finely ground Turkish coffee
1 teaspoon (4 grams) sugar (optional)
1 cardamom pod (optional)

INSTRUCTIONS:

Combine water, coffee, sugar (if using), and cardamom (if using) in a Turkish coffee pot or small saucepan.
Stir well to dissolve the coffee and sugar. Place the pot over low heat and allow the coffee to heat slowly without stirring.
When coffee begins to froth and bubble, carefully remove it from the heat. Let the coffee settle, then pour it into a serving cup, allowing the grounds to remain in the pot. Serve immediately.

FLAVORED SYRUPS

Flavored syrups are luscious elixirs infused with a wide spectrum of delightful tastes, meticulously crafted to elevate beverages and dishes. These syrups come in an extensive array of flavors, from timeless classics like vanilla and chocolate to unique and exotic options such as lavender and gingerbread. With their ability to effortlessly enhance the flavor profile of coffee, cocktails, teas, and desserts, flavored syrups have become a cherished secret ingredient in the culinary world. Whether drizzled over pancakes, blended into a latte, or mixed into cocktails, these syrups offer a quick and accessible way to infuse dishes with an extra layer of indulgence and creativity.

CLASSIC SYRUP

Prep Time: 5 Min

Serving: 1

INGREDIENTS:

1 cup (240 mL) water
1 cup (200 g) granulated sugar

INSTRUCTIONS:

Add sugar and water to a saucepan. Warm over medium heat until the sugar is fully dissolved. Bring to a gentle boil, then reduce heat, and let it simmer for 3 minutes. Remove the pan from the heat and allow the syrup to cool. Transfer the cooled syrup into a clean container for storage

VANILLA SYRUP

Prep Time: 5 Min

Serving: 1

INGREDIENTS:

1 cup (240 mL) water
1 cup (200 g) sugar
2 vanilla beans (for strong flavor)

INSTRUCTIONS:

Add sugar and water to a saucepan and heat over medium heat, stirring occasionally.
Split the vanilla beans, scrape the seeds, and add both seeds and the pod to the saucepan.
Simmer this mixture for 10 minutes to infuse the vanilla flavor.
Remove the pan, let it cool completely, then strain into a clean bottle.

HAZELNUT SYRUP

Prep Time: 10 Min

Serving: 1

INGREDIENTS:

1 cup (240 mL) water
1 cup (200 g) sugar
1 cup (approx. 145 g) crushed hazelnuts

INSTRUCTIONS:

Toast hazelnuts lightly, then crush them to release their oils.
Combine the crushed hazelnuts, sugar, and water in a saucepan.
Simmer the mixture for about 10 minutes, allowing the hazelnut flavor to infuse.
Let it cool, then strain the syrup, discarding the hazelnuts.

COCONUT SYRUP

Prep Time:
5 Min

Serving:
1

INGREDIENTS:

1 cup (200 grams) granulated sugar
1 cup (240 milliliters) water
1 cup (85 grams) shredded coconut

INSTRUCTIONS:

Combine the sugar, water, and shredded coconut in a saucepan over medium heat. Stir until the sugar is completely dissolved. Bring to a gentle boil and simmer for 10 minutes. Remove from heat and allow to cool. Strain the syrup, discard the shredded coconut, and store in a clean container.

LAVENDER SYRUP

Prep Time: 5 Min

Serving: 1

INGREDIENTS:

1 cup (240 mL) water
1 cup (200 g) sugar
2 tbsp (approx. 3.6 g) dried lavender

INSTRUCTIONS:

Add water, sugar, and dried lavender to a saucepan and gently heat.
Allow the mixture to simmer lightly for about 10-15 minutes.
Remove it from the heat and let it cool, letting the lavender infuse its flavor.
Strain the syrup, remove the lavender pieces, and store it in a clean bottle.

PUMPKIN SPICE SYRUP

Prep Time: 5 Min

Serving: 1

INGREDIENTS:

1 cup (240 ml) water
1 cup (200 g) sugar
2 tbsp (30 g) pumpkin puree
1 tsp (5 g) ground cinnamon
1/2 tsp (2.5 g) ground nutmeg
1/2 tsp (2.5 g) ground ginger

INSTRUCTIONS:

Add all ingredients into a saucepan and bring to a simmer. Then cook it for 10 minutes, stirring occasionally. Remove the pan and let it cool.
Strain the syrup using a fine-mesh sieve into a clean bottle for storage.

CARAMEL BRULÉE SYRUP

Prep Time: 5 Min

Serving: 1

INGREDIENTS:

1 cup (150 g) white chocolate chips
1/2 cup (120 ml) heavy cream

INSTRUCTIONS:

Add heavy cream to a saucepan and gently warm over low heat. Add white chocolate chips to the cream, stirring continuously until fully melted. Remove the saucepan from the heat once the mixture is smooth and combined. Cool thoroughly before transferring it to a container for storage.

ALMOND SYRUP

Prep Time: 5 Min

Serving: 1

INGREDIENTS:

1 cup (200 g) granulated sugar
1 cup (240 ml) water
½ cup (70 g) raw almonds, finely chopped

INSTRUCTIONS:

Add sugar and water into the pan (enough to hold the ingredients) and boil until the sugar dissolves.
Add chopped almonds, reducing heat, and simmer for 5 minutes.
Remove the pan, cover, and let it steep for at least 10 minutes.
Strain the syrup, discard the almonds, and let it cool before storage.

COCONUT SYRUP

Prep Time: 5 Min

Serving: 1

INGREDIENTS:

1 cup (200 g) granulated sugar
1 cup (240 ml) coconut milk
1 tsp (5 ml) vanilla extract

INSTRUCTIONS:

Add sugar and coconut milk in a saucepan, stirring over medium heat until sugar dissolves.
Boil this mixture, then reduce heat to simmer for about 5 minutes.
Remove the pan and stir in the vanilla extract.
Cool the syrup before transferring it to a container for storage.

RASPBERRY SYRUP

Prep Time:
10 Min

Serving:
1

INGREDIENTS:

1 cup (125 g) fresh raspberries
1 cup (200 g) granulated sugar
1 cup (240 ml) water

INSTRUCTIONS:

Add raspberries, sugar, and water in a saucepan. Bring it to a boil.
Decrease the stove heat and let it simmer for 15-20 minutes, allowing the raspberries to break down.
Strain the mixture to discard seeds and pulp, retaining the syrup.
Cool the syrup before pouring it into a clean container for storage.

TOFFEE NUT SYRUP

Prep Time: 5 Min

Serving: 1

INGREDIENTS:

1 cup (200 g) granulated sugar
1 cup (220 g) brown sugar
1 cup (240 ml) water
1 tsp (5 ml) vanilla extract

INSTRUCTIONS:

Combine sugars and water in a saucepan over medium heat, stirring until sugars dissolve.
Bring to a boil, then decrease the heat and simmer for 7-10 minutes or until it thickens slightly. Remove from heat, stir in vanilla extract.
Cool the syrup before transferring it to a storage container.

SALTED CARAMEL SYRUP

Prep Time: 5 Min

Serving: 1

INGREDIENTS:

1 cup (200 g) granulated sugar
½ cup (120 ml) water
½ cup (120 ml) heavy cream
1 tsp (5 g) sea salt

INSTRUCTIONS:

Add sugar and water in a saucepan over medium heat, stirring until sugar dissolves. Increase heat and boil the mixture. Let it cook without stirring until it turns amber in color.
Remove the pan, and slowly whisk in heavy cream until smooth.
Stir in sea salt and allow the syrup to cool before pouring it into a storage container.

CLASSIC FLAVORED LATTES

Experience the timeless fusion of coffee and flavor in our Classic Flavored Lattes. Delight in well-loved combinations from creamy vanilla to rich mocha, and rediscover why these lattes remain perennial favorites. Dive in and savor each sip.

VANILLA LATTE

Prep Time: 5 Min

Serving: 1

INGREDIENTS:

1 shot (30 milliliters) espresso
1 cup (240 milliliters) whole milk
1 teaspoon (5 milliliters) vanilla syrup
whipped cream for garnish (optional)

INSTRUCTIONS:

Brew a shot of espresso and pour into a mug. Heat and froth the milk, adding Vanilla Syrup as it heats.
Pour the frothy vanilla milk over the espresso. Garnish with whipped cream and serve immediately.

HAZELNUT LATTE

Prep Time: 5 Min

Serving: 1

INGREDIENTS:

1 shot (30 milliliters) espresso
1 cup (240 milliliters) whole milk
1 teaspoon (5 milliliters) hazelnut syrup
whipped cream and chopped hazelnuts for garnish (optional)

INSTRUCTIONS:

Brew a shot of espresso into a mug. Heat and froth milk with Hazelnut Syrup. Pour frothy hazelnut milk over espresso.
Garnish with whipped cream and chopped hazelnuts if desired, then serve.

MOCHA LATTE

Prep Time: 5 Min

Serving: 1

INGREDIENTS:

1 shot (30 milliliters) espresso
1 cup (240 milliliters) whole milk
1 tablespoon (15 milliliters) chocolate sauce

INSTRUCTIONS:

Brew the 1 shot espresso, then pour it into the mug. Heat and froth milk with Chocolate Sauce until well mixed.
Pour chocolate milk over espresso. Serve and enjoy.

COCONUT MOCHA LATTE

Prep Time: 5 Min

Serving: 1

INGREDIENTS:

1 shot (30 milliliters) espresso
1 cup (240 milliliters) milk
2 tablespoons (30 milliliters) coconut syrup
1 tablespoon (15 milliliters) chocolate syrup

INSTRUCTIONS:

Brew the espresso shot and pour it into a mug.
In a separate container, heat the milk until it's warm but not boiling.
Froth the milk and then add it to the mug with the espresso.
Stir in the coconut syrup and chocolate syrup.
Optionally, garnish with whipped cream and a sprinkle of shredded coconut or chocolate shavings.
Enjoy!

WHITE CHOCOLATE MOCHA

Prep Time: 5 Min

Serving: 1

INGREDIENTS:

1 shot (30 milliliters) espresso
1 cup (240 milliliters) whole milk
1 tablespoon (15 milliliters) white chocolate sauce

INSTRUCTIONS:

Brew espresso and pour it into a mug. Heat and froth milk with White Chocolate Sauce. Pour the mixture over espresso.
Serve immediately. Feel free to adjust the quantity of syrups in each recipe to suit your taste preferences.
Each recipe can be further customized with different types of milk, additional toppings, or served over ice for a refreshing iced beverage version.

CARAMEL MACCHIATO

Prep Time: 5 Min

Serving: 1

INGREDIENTS:

1 shot (30 milliliters) espresso
1 cup (240 milliliters) whole milk
1 tablespoon (15 millilitres) caramel sauce
whipped cream and additional caramel sauce for garnish (optional)

INSTRUCTIONS:

Brew a shot of espresso and pour into a mug. Heat and froth milk, then pour it over the espresso.
Drizzle caramel sauce over the frothy milk. Optional: garnish with whipped cream and an additional drizzle of caramel sauce, then serve.

CAFÉ MIEL LATTE

Prep Time: 5 Min

Serving: 1

INGREDIENTS:

1 shot (30 milliliters) espresso
1 cup (240 milliliters) whole milk
1 teaspoon (5 milliliters) honey
1/4 teaspoon (1.25 millilitres) vanilla extract
dash of ground cinnamon

INSTRUCTIONS:

Brew the espresso shot and pour it into a mug. Heat milk, honey, and vanilla until warm and frothy.
Pour the frothy milk mixture over the espresso. Sprinkle with cinnamon and serve immediately.

MAPLE LATTE

Prep Time: 5 Min

Serving: 1

INGREDIENTS:

1 shot (30 milliliters) espresso
1 cup (240 milliliters) whole milk
1 tablespoon (15 milliliters) pure maple syrup
Whipped cream to garnish (optional)

INSTRUCTIONS:

Brew the espresso shot and pour it into a mug.
Heat and froth milk with maple syrup.
Pour the frothy maple milk over the espresso.
Garnish with whipped cream if desired, then serve.

COCONUT LATTE

Prep Time: 5 Min

Serving: 1

INGREDIENTS:

1 shot (30 milliliters) espresso
1 cup (240 milliliters) coconut milk
1 teaspoon (5 milliliters) Classic Syrup
Toasted coconut flakes for garnish (optional)

INSTRUCTIONS:

Brew the espresso shot and pour it into a mug.
Heat and froth coconut milk with Classic Syrup.
Pour the frothy coconut milk over the espresso.
Garnish with toasted coconut flakes if desired, and serve immediately.

MATCHA LATTE

Prep Time: 5 Min

Serving: 1

INGREDIENTS:

1 teaspoon (5 grams) matcha powder
1 cup (240 milliliters) whole milk
1 teaspoon (5 milliliters) Vanilla Syrup
Whipped cream for garnish (optional)

INSTRUCTIONS:

Sift matcha powder into a mug.
Heat and froth milk with Vanilla Syrup.
Pour the frothy vanilla milk over matcha, whisking until smooth.
Optional: Garnish with whipped cream and serve immediately.

PISTACHIO LATTE

Prep Time: 5 Min

Serving: 1

INGREDIENTS:

1 shot (30 milliliters) espresso
1 cup (240 milliliters) whole milk
1 tbsp (5 millilitres) Pistachio Syrup
Whipped cream to garnish (optional)

INSTRUCTIONS:

Brew a shot of espresso and pour into a mug.
Heat and froth milk, incorporating Pistachio Syrup as it warms.
Pour frothy pistachio milk over the espresso.
Garnish with whipped cream if desired, then serve.

TIRAMISU LATTE

Prep Time: 5 Min

Serving: 1

INGREDIENTS:

1 shot (30 milliliters) espresso
1 cup (240 milliliters) whole milk
1 teaspoon (5 milliliters) Vanilla Syrup
1 teaspoon (5 milliliters) Chocolate Sauce
Whipped cream and cocoa powder to Top (optional)

INSTRUCTIONS:

Brew the espresso shot and pour it into a mug.
Heat and froth milk with Vanilla Syrup and Chocolate Sauce.
Pour the frothy mixture over the espresso.
Top with whipped cream and sprinkle cocoa powder if desired, then serve.

SPICED CHAI LATTE

Prep Time: 5 Min

Serving: 1

INGREDIENTS:

1 cup (240 milliliters) whole milk
1 spiced chai tea bag or 1 teaspoon (5 grams) loose chai tea
1 shot (30 milliliters) espresso (optional for a "dirty" chai latte)
1 teaspoon (5 milliliters) Classic Syrup
Whipped cream and cinnamon powder for garnish (optional)

INSTRUCTIONS:

Heat milk until warm and steep chai tea for 3-5 minutes, then put out the tea bag or strain loose tea.
Brew the espresso shot and pour it into a mug if making a "dirty" chai latte.
Sweeten chai milk with Classic Syrup and pour over espresso (or pour alone for a traditional chai latte).
Garnish with whipped cream and a sprinkle cinnamon powder if desired, then serve.

ARTISANAL FLAVORED LATTES

Venture beyond the familiar and explore the artistry of flavor infusion in our Artisanal Lattes. With unique blends like rosemary honey and maple sage, every sip is an adventure. Dive in and let these crafted concoctions enchant your palate.

LAVENDER VANILLA LATTE

Prep Time: 5 Min

Serving: 1

INGREDIENTS:

1 shot (30 milliliters) espresso
1 cup (240 milliliters) whole milk
1/2 teaspoon dried lavender buds
1/2 teaspoon vanilla extract

INSTRUCTIONS:

Brew a shot of espresso and pour into a mug.
Heat milk with lavender buds until warm, then strain to remove buds.
Stir in vanilla extract and froth the milk.
Pour the frothy milk over the espresso and serve.

PUMPKIN CARDAMOM LATTE

Prep Time: 5 Min

Serving: 1

INGREDIENTS:

1 shot (30 milliliters) espresso
1 cup (240 milliliters) whole milk
2 tablespoons pumpkin puree
1/4 teaspoon ground cardamom
1 teaspoon honey

INSTRUCTIONS:

Brew a shot of espresso and pour into a mug.
Heat milk, pumpkin puree, cardamom, and honey, whisking until well mixed and warm.
Froth the pumpkin milk and pour over the espresso.
Serve warm with a sprinkle of cardamom on top.

MAPLE SAGE LATTE

Prep Time: 5 Min

Serving: 1

INGREDIENTS:

1 shot (30 milliliters) espresso
1 cup (240 milliliters) whole milk
1 tablespoon pure maple syrup
1/2 teaspoon dried sage

INSTRUCTIONS:

Brew the espresso shot and pour it into a mug.
Heat milk with sage until warm, then strain to remove sage.
Stir in maple syrup, froth the milk, and pour over the espresso.
Serve immediately with a sprinkle of ground sage if desired.

ORANGE MOCHA

Prep Time: 5 Min

Serving: 1

INGREDIENTS:

1 shot (30 milliliters) espresso
1 cup (240 milliliters) whole milk
1 tablespoon chocolate syrup
1/2 teaspoon orange zest

INSTRUCTIONS:

Brew the espresso shot and pour it into a mug.
Heat milk with chocolate syrup and orange zest until well-mixed and warm.
Froth the chocolate milk and pour over the espresso.
Garnish with extra orange zest and serve warm.

CINNAMON ROLL LATTE

Prep Time: 5 Min

Serving: 1

INGREDIENTS:

1 shot (30 milliliters) espresso
1 cup (240 milliliters) whole milk
1/2 teaspoon ground cinnamon
1 tablespoon brown sugar

INSTRUCTIONS:

Brew the espresso shot and pour it into a mug.
Heat milk with cinnamon and brown sugar until the sugar is dissolved and the milk is warm.
Froth the cinnamon milk and pour over the espresso.
Serve warm.

SPICY MEXICAN MOCHA

Prep Time: 5 Min

Serving: 1

INGREDIENTS:

1 shot (30 milliliters) espresso
1 cup (240 milliliters) whole milk
1 tablespoon cocoa powder
1/2 teaspoon cinnamon
Pinch of cayenne pepper

INSTRUCTIONS:

Brew the 1 espresso shot and pour it into a mug.
Heat milk with cocoa powder, cinnamon, and cayenne until warm and well-mixed.
Froth the spicy chocolate milk and pour over the espresso.
Serve with a sprinkle of cinnamon on top.

TURMERIC GINGER LATTE

Prep Time: 5 Min

Serving: 1

INGREDIENTS:

1 shot (30 milliliters) espresso
1 cup (240 milliliters) whole milk
1/2 teaspoon ground turmeric
1/4 teaspoon ground ginger

INSTRUCTIONS:

Brew the espresso shot and pour it into a mug.
Heat milk with turmeric and ginger until warm.
Froth the milk and pour over the espresso.
Serve immediately with a sprinkle of turmeric and ginger.

NUTELLA LATTE

Prep Time: 5 Min

Serving: 1

INGREDIENTS:

1 shot (30 milliliters) espresso
1 cup (240 milliliters) whole milk
1 tablespoon Nutella

INSTRUCTIONS:

Brew the espresso shot and pour it into a mug.
Heat milk and Nutella until warm and well-mixed.
Froth the Nutella milk and pour over the espresso.
Serve warm topped with whipped cream, if desired.

BROWN SUGAR LATTE

Prep Time: 5 Min

Serving: 1

INGREDIENTS:

1 shot (30 milliliters) espresso
1 cup (240 milliliters) whole milk
1 tablespoon brown sugar

INSTRUCTIONS:

Brew the espresso shot and pour it into a mug.
Heat milk with brown sugar until the sugar is dissolved and the milk is warm.
Froth the milk and pour over the espresso.
Serve immediately.

HONEY LATTE

Prep Time: 5 Min

Serving: 1

INGREDIENTS:

1 shot (30 milliliters) espresso
1 cup (240 milliliters) whole milk
1 tablespoon honey

INSTRUCTIONS:

Brew the 1 espresso shot and pour it into a mug.
Heat milk and honey until warm and well-mixed.
Froth the honey milk and pour over the espresso.
Drizzle honey on top.
Serve immediately.

BUTTERSCOTCH LATTE

Prep Time: 5 Min

Serving: 1

INGREDIENTS:

1 shot (30 milliliters) espresso
1 cup (240 milliliters) whole milk
1 tablespoon butterscotch sauce

INSTRUCTIONS:

Brew a shot of espresso and pour into a mug.
Heat the milk and butterscotch sauce, stirring until the sauce is fully dissolved.
Froth the butterscotch milk mixture and pour over the espresso.
Top with whipped cream and a drizzle of butterscotch sauce, then serve immediately.

THAI LATTE

Prep Time: 5 Min

Serving: 1

INGREDIENTS:

1 shot (30 milliliters) espresso
1/2 cup (120 milliliters) whole milk
1/2 cup (120 milliliters) sweetened condensed milk

INSTRUCTIONS:

Brew a shot of espresso and pour into a mug.
Heat whole and sweetened condensed milk in a saucepan, stirring until combined and warm.
Froth the milk mixture slightly and pour over the espresso.
Serve warm with a sprinkle of cinnamon powder or nutmeg, if desired.

S'MORES LATTE

Prep Time: 5 Min

Serving: 1

INGREDIENTS:

1 shot (30 milliliters) espresso
1 cup (240 milliliters) whole milk
1 tablespoon chocolate syrup
Whipped cream, graham cracker crumbs, and mini marshmallows for garnish

INSTRUCTIONS:

Brew a shot of espresso and pour into a mug.
Heat the milk and chocolate syrup until warm and well-mixed.
Froth the chocolate milk and pour over the espresso.
Top with whipped cream, a sprinkle of graham cracker crumbs, and mini marshmallows. Optionally, you can use a kitchen torch to toast the marshmallows lightly.
Serve immediately and enjoy the delightful taste of a classic treat in latte form.

HOLIDAY INSPIRED LATTES

Celebrate the seasons with lattes inspired by festive flavors. From the warmth of pumpkin spice to the joy of peppermint bark, these drinks encapsulate the spirit of holidays. Dive in and let each latte bring festive cheer to your cup.

PUMPKIN SPICE LATTE

Prep Time: 5 Min

Serving: 1

INGREDIENTS:

1 shot (30 milliliters) espresso
1 cup (240 milliliters) whole milk
2 tablespoons pumpkin puree
1/2 teaspoon pumpkin pie spice

INSTRUCTIONS:

Brew a shot of espresso and pour into a mug.
Heat milk, pumpkin puree, and pumpkin pie spice until warm.
Froth the pumpkin milk mixture and pour over the espresso.
Serve warm with a sprinkle of pumpkin pie spice on top.

GINGERBREAD LATTE

Prep Time: 5 Min

Serving: 1

INGREDIENTS:

1 shot (30 milliliters) espresso
1 cup (240 milliliters) whole milk
1/2 teaspoon ground ginger
1/2 teaspoon ground cinnamon

INSTRUCTIONS:

Brew the espresso shot and
Pour into the serving mug. Heat milk with ginger and cinnamon until warm.
Froth the milk and pour over the espresso.
Serve warm with cinnamon on top.

CANDY CANE LATTE

Prep Time: 5 Min

Serving: 1

INGREDIENTS:

1 shot (30 milliliters) espresso
1 cup (240 milliliters) whole milk
1 peppermint candy cane, crushed

INSTRUCTIONS:

Brew a shot of espresso and pour into a mug.
Heat milk and half of the crushed candy cane until the candy is dissolved and the milk is warm.
Froth the peppermint milk and pour over the espresso.
Garnish with whipped cream and the remaining crushed candy cane, then serve.

EGGNOG LATTE

Prep Time: 5 Min

Serving: 1

INGREDIENTS:

1 shot (30 milliliters) espresso
1/2 cup (120 milliliters) whole milk
1/2 cup (120 milliliters) eggnog

INSTRUCTIONS:

Brew the espresso shot and pour into the serving mug.
Heat milk and eggnog until warm, being careful not to boil.
Froth the eggnog milk mixture and pour over the espresso.
Garnish with a sprinkle of nutmeg, then serve.

HOLIDAY SPICE LATTE

Prep Time: 5 Min

Serving: 1

INGREDIENTS:

1 shot (30 milliliters) espresso
1 cup (240 milliliters) whole milk
1/4 teaspoon ground cinnamon
1/8 teaspoon ground nutmeg
1/8 teaspoon ground cloves

INSTRUCTIONS:

Brew the espresso shot and pour into the mug.
Heat milk with cinnamon, nutmeg, and cloves until warm.
Froth the spiced milk and pour over the espresso.
Serve warm, and sprinkle cinnamon on top.

VALENTINE'S CARDAMOM ROSE LATTE

Prep Time: 5 Min

Serving: 1

INGREDIENTS:

1 shot (30 milliliters) espresso
1 cup (240 milliliters) whole milk
1/2 teaspoon ground cardamom
1/2 teaspoon rose water

INSTRUCTIONS:

Brew a shot of espresso and pour into a mug.
Heat milk with cardamom until warm.
Stir in rose water and froth the milk.
Pour frothy milk over the espresso and serve with rose petals as garnish if desired.

THANKSGIVING APPLE PIE LATTE

Prep Time: 5 Min

Serving: 1

INGREDIENTS:

1 shot (30 milliliters) espresso
1 cup (240 milliliters) apple cider
1/2 teaspoon ground cinnamon

INSTRUCTIONS:

Brew a shot of espresso and pour into a mug.
Heat apple cider with cinnamon until warm.
Froth the cider slightly and pour over the espresso.
Serve warm, and sprinkle of cinnamon on top.

CHRISTMAS PEPPERMINT MOCHA

Prep Time: 5 Min

Serving: 1

INGREDIENTS:

1 shot (30 milliliters) espresso
1 cup (240 milliliters) whole milk
1 tablespoon (15 milliliters) chocolate sauce
1 teaspoon (5 millilitres) peppermint syrup

INSTRUCTIONS:

Brew the one espresso shot and pour it into a mug. Heat milk, Chocolate Sauce, and Peppermint Syrup, then froth.
Pour the frothy milk mixture over the espresso.

CRANBERRY BLISS LATTE

Prep Time: 5 Min

Serving: 1

INGREDIENTS:

1 shot (30 milliliters) espresso
1 cup (240 milliliters) whole milk
1 tablespoon cranberry sauce
1 teaspoon honey

INSTRUCTIONS:

Brew a shot of espresso and pour into a mug.
Heat milk, honey and cranberry sauce until the sauce is dissolved and the milk is warm.
Froth the milk and pour over the espresso.
Serve warm with whipped cream and dried cranberries as garnish.

WINTER WONDERLAND LATTE

Prep Time: 5 Min

Serving: 1

INGREDIENTS:

1 shot (30 milliliters) espresso
1 cup (240 milliliters) coconut milk
1 tablespoon white chocolate chips

INSTRUCTIONS:

Brew the espresso shot and pour it into a mug.
Heat coconut milk and white chocolate chips until the chocolate is melted and the mixture is warm. Froth the milk and pour over the espresso.
Garnish with whipped cream and shredded coconut, then serve immediately.

SPICED ORANGE LATTE

Prep Time: 5 Min

Serving: 1

INGREDIENTS:

1 shot (30 milliliters) espresso
1 cup (240 milliliters) whole milk
1 tablespoon orange marmalade
1/4 teaspoon ground cinnamon

INSTRUCTIONS:

Brew a shot of espresso and pour into a mug.
Heat milk, orange marmalade, and cinnamon, stirring until the mixture is dissolved and warm.
Froth the milk and pour over the espresso.
Garnish with a sprinkle of cinnamon and a twist of orange zest, then serve warm.

MAPLE PECAN PIE LATTE

Prep Time: 5 Min

Serving: 1

INGREDIENTS:

1 shot (30 milliliters) espresso
1 cup (240 milliliters) whole milk
1 teaspoon (5 millilitres) maple syrup (if available, or use classic syrup)
1 teaspoon (5 millilitres) of pecan syrup (if available)
whipped cream and chopped pecans for garnish

INSTRUCTIONS:

Brew the shot of espresso and ladle it into a mug. Heat and froth milk with Maple and Pecan Syrup. Pour the frothy milk over the espresso.
Top with whipped cream and chopped pecans, then serve.

CHERRY BLOSSOM LATTE

Prep Time: 5 Min

Serving: 1

INGREDIENTS:

1 shot (30 milliliters) espresso
1 cup (240 milliliters) whole milk
1 teaspoon cherry syrup
Pink food coloring (optional)

INSTRUCTIONS:

First, brew the espresso shot and pour it into a mug.
Heat milk with cherry syrup and optional food coloring until the syrup is dissolved and the mixture is warm.
Froth the milk, then pour over the espresso.
Top with whipped cream and a maraschino cherry, then serve immediately.

ICED FLAVORED LATTES

Cool down and refresh with our Iced Flavored Lattes. Perfect for sunny days, these chilled brews combine invigorating coffee with delightful flavors. Dive in and experience the bliss of a cold, flavor-packed sip.

ICED BROWN SUGAR OAT MILK LATTE

Prep Time: 5 Min

Serving: 1

INGREDIENTS:

1 shot (30 milliliters) espresso
1 cup (240 milliliters) oat milk
1 tablespoon brown sugar

INSTRUCTIONS:

Brew a shot of espresso and allow it to cool slightly.
While it's cooling, dissolve brown sugar in the espresso.
In a glass, add ice, and pour the sweetened espresso over.
Top the glass with cold oat milk, gently stir, and serve immediately.

ICED SALTED HONEY LATTE

Prep Time: 5 Min

Serving: 1

INGREDIENTS:

1 shot (30 milliliters) espresso
1 cup (240 milliliters) whole milk
1 tablespoon honey
Pinch of sea salt

INSTRUCTIONS:

Prepare a shot of espresso and let it cool.
In the cooled espresso, dissolve the honey and add a pinch of sea salt.
Pour the espresso over a glass of ice, followed by cold milk.
Stir well to combine and serve immediately.

ICED HONEY LAVENDER LATTE

Prep Time: 5 Min

Serving: 1

INGREDIENTS:

1 shot (30 milliliters) espresso
1 cup (240 milliliters) whole milk
1 tablespoon honey
1/4 teaspoon lavender extract

INSTRUCTIONS:

Brew espresso and allow it to cool.
Mix honey and lavender extract into the cooled espresso.
Pour the espresso into a glass with ice and top with cold milk.
Gently stir and serve immediately.

ICED DIRTY CHAI LATTE

Prep Time: 5 Min

Serving: 1

INGREDIENTS:

1 shot (30 milliliters) espresso
1 cup (240 milliliters) cold chai tea
1/2 cup (120 milliliters) whole milk

INSTRUCTIONS:

Brew and cool a shot of espresso.
In a glass, add ice, and pour the cooled espresso.
Add the cold chai tea and top with milk.
Stir gently and serve immediately.

ICED CINNAMON DOLCE LATTE

Prep Time: 5 Min

Serving: 1

INGREDIENTS:

1 shot (30 milliliters) espresso
1 cup (240 milliliters) whole milk
1 tablespoon cinnamon syrup

INSTRUCTIONS:

Brew a shot of espresso and allow it to cool.
Into the cooled espresso, mix in the cinnamon syrup.
Fill a glass with ice and pour the sweetened espresso over it.
Top with cold milk, gently stir and serve immediately.

ICED TOFFEE NUT LATTE

Prep Time: 5 Min

Serving: 1

INGREDIENTS:

1 shot (30 milliliters) espresso
1 cup (240 milliliters) whole milk
1 tablespoon toffee nut syrup

INSTRUCTIONS:

Brew a shot of espresso and allow it to cool slightly.
Mix in the toffee nut syrup.
Pour the sweetened espresso into a glass filled with ice.
Top with cold milk and serve immediately.

ICED CARAMEL BRULÉE LATTE

Prep Time: 5 Min

Serving: 1

INGREDIENTS:

1 shot (30 milliliters) espresso
1 cup (240 milliliters) whole milk
1 tablespoon caramel Brulée syrup

INSTRUCTIONS:

Brew the one-shot espresso and let it cool.
Add caramel Brulée syrup to the espresso and mix.
Add ice into the serving glass and pour the sweetened espresso over it.
Top with cold milk, stir slightly and serve.

ICED VANILLA SWEET CREAM LATTE

Prep Time: 5 Min

Serving: 1

INGREDIENTS:

1 shot (30 milliliters) espresso
½ cup (120 milliliters) cold milk
½ cup (120 milliliters) ice cubes
1 teaspoon (5 milliliters) vanilla syrup
¼ cup (60 milliliters) heavy cream

INSTRUCTIONS:

Brew the espresso shot and let it cool slightly. Add ice cubes into the glass and pour the espresso over the ice. In a separate container, mix the cold milk and vanilla syrup well. Pour the vanilla milk over the iced espresso, mixing gently.
In the other bowl, whisk the heavy cream until it thickens slightly, creating a creamy texture. Top the iced latte with the whipped sweet cream. Stir gently before sipping, or enjoy the layers of flavor individually. Enjoy your refreshing Iced Vanilla Sweet Cream Latte!

ICED PUMPKIN COLD BREW LATTE

Prep Time: 10 Min

Serving: 1

INGREDIENTS:

1 cup (240 milliliters) cold brew coffee
¼ cup (60 milliliters) pumpkin puree
2 tablespoons (30 milliliters) vanilla syrup
½ teaspoon (2.5 milliliters) pumpkin pie spice
½ cup (120 milliliters) of milk for cold foam
Ice cubes

INSTRUCTIONS:

Prepare the cold brew coffee in advance; it needs time to brew.
Mix cold brew, pumpkin puree, vanilla syrup, and pumpkin pie spice until well combined. Add ice cubes into the serving glass and pour the mixed ingredients over the ice. Froth the milk until it's creamy and thick, then gently layer the cold foam over the coffee. Stir gently before enjoying your refreshing Iced Pumpkin Cold Brew Latte.

ICED HONEY CINNAMON LATTE

Prep Time: 5 Min

Serving: 1

INGREDIENTS:

1 cup (240 milliliters) cold brew coffee
2 tablespoons (30 milliliters) honey syrup
1/2 teaspoon (2.5 milliliters) cinnamon, ground
1/2 cup (120 milliliters) of milk for cold foam
Ice cubes as needed

INSTRUCTIONS:

Combine cold brew coffee, honey syrup, and ground cinnamon in a glass.
Fill the glass with ice cubes as per preference.
Froth the milk until it's creamy and has a cold foam consistency.
Gently pour the cold foam over the iced coffee mixture.
Stir gently before serving, and enjoy your refreshing Iced Honey Cinnamon Latte.

ICED SALTED MAPLE COLD BREW LATTE

Prep Time: 5 Min

Serving: 1

INGREDIENTS:

1 cup (240 milliliters) cold brew coffee
2 tablespoons (30 milliliters) maple syrup
1/4 teaspoon (1.25 milliliters) sea salt
1/2 cup (120 milliliters) of milk for cold foam
Ice cubes as needed

INSTRUCTIONS:

Mix cold brew coffee with maple syrup and sea salt in a glass.
Add your preferred amount of ice cubes to the glass.
Froth the milk until it achieves a cold foam consistency and is ready to serve.
Top your iced coffee mix with the cold foam milk gently.
Mix slightly and savor your delicious Iced Salted Maple Cold Brew Latte.

ICED RASPBERRY MOCHA

Prep Time: 5 Min

Serving: 1

INGREDIENTS:

1 cup (240 milliliters) cold brew coffee
2 tablespoons (30 milliliters) chocolate syrup
2 tablespoons (30 milliliters) raspberry syrup
1/2 cup (120 milliliters) of milk for cold foam
Ice cubes as needed

INSTRUCTIONS:

Mix cold brewed coffee with chocolate and raspberry syrups in a serving glass.
Introduce as many ice cubes as you prefer into the mixture.
Froth milk until it turns into a cold, creamy foam.
Delicately pour the cold foam over the iced mocha mixture in the glass.
Gently stir the concoction and enjoy your delightful Iced Raspberry Mocha.

BLENDED COFFEE DRINKS

Embrace the creamy fusion of coffee, ice, and flavors in our Blended Coffee Drinks. These frosty delights offer both refreshment and a caffeine kick. Dive in and discover the perfect blend of texture and taste in every sip.

CLASSIC FRAPPUCCINO

Prep Time: 5 Min

Serving: 1

INGREDIENTS:

1 cup (240 milliliters) brewed coffee, cooled
1/2 cup (120 milliliters) milk
2 cups ice
3 tablespoons sugar

INSTRUCTIONS:

Combine cooled coffee, milk, ice, and sugar in a blender.
Blend until smooth and frothy.
Pour into a glass and serve immediately.
Top with whipped cream if desired.

CREAMY COFFEE SMOOTHIE

Prep Time: 5 Min

Serving: 1

INGREDIENTS:

1 banana
1 cup (240 milliliters) brewed coffee, cooled
1/2 cup (120 milliliters) Greek yogurt
1 tablespoon honey

INSTRUCTIONS:

Place banana, cooled coffee, Greek yogurt, and honey in a blender.
Blend until smooth.
Pour into a glass and serve immediately.
Garnish with a drizzle of honey or a slice of banana if desired.

MOCHA FRAPPUCCINO

Prep Time: 5 Min

Serving: 1

INGREDIENTS:

1 cup (240 milliliters) brewed coffee, cooled
1/2 cup (120 milliliters) milk
2 cups ice
2 tablespoons chocolate syrup

INSTRUCTIONS:

Combine cooled coffee, milk, ice, and chocolate syrup in a blender.
Blend until smooth and frothy.
Pour into the serving glass and serve with whipped cream if desired.

CARAMEL FRAPPUCCINO

Prep Time: 5 Min

Serving: 1

INGREDIENTS:

1 cup (240 milliliters) brewed coffee, cooled
1/2 cup (120 milliliters) milk
2 cups ice
2 tablespoons caramel syrup

INSTRUCTIONS:

Mix cooled coffee, milk, ice, and caramel syrup in a blender.
Blend until smooth and creamy.
Pour into the serving glass and top with whipped cream and extra caramel syrup.

JAVA CHIP FRAPPUCCINO

Prep Time: 5 Min

Serving: 1

INGREDIENTS:

1 cup (240 milliliters) brewed coffee, cooled
1/2 cup (120 milliliters) milk
2 cups ice
2 tablespoons chocolate syrup
1/4 cup chocolate chips

INSTRUCTIONS:

Combine cooled coffee, milk, ice, chocolate syrup, and chocolate chips in a blender. Blend until the mixture is smooth.
Pour into the glass and top with whipped cream and extra chocolate chips or chocolate syrup.

COCONUT MILK MOCHA MACCHIATO FRAPPUCCINO

Prep Time: 5 Min

Serving: 1

INGREDIENTS:

1 cup (240 milliliters) strong brewed coffee, chilled
1/2 cup (120 milliliters) coconut milk
2 tablespoons (30 milliliters) chocolate syrup
2 tablespoons (30 milliliters) caramel syrup
1 cup (240 milliliters) ice cubes

INSTRUCTIONS:

Combine the chilled coffee, coconut milk, and ice cubes in a blender. Blend until smooth and icy. Drizzle the inside of your serving glass with chocolate syrup.
Pour the blended coffee into the prepared glass.
Drizzle caramel syrup over the top of the blended coffee.
Optionally, garnish with whipped cream and a sprinkle of cocoa or a drizzle of more syrup. Enjoy immediately.

WHITE CHOCOLATE MOCHA FRAPPUCCINO

Prep Time: 5 Min

Serving: 1

INGREDIENTS:

1 cup (240 milliliters) cold brewed coffee
2 cups ice
2 tbsp (30 milliliters) white chocolate syrup.
1/4 cup (60 milliliters) milk

INSTRUCTIONS:

Blend coffee, ice, white chocolate syrup, and milk until smooth.
Pour into a glass and serve.
Optional: top with whipped cream and white chocolate drizzle.

STRAWBERRIES AND CRÈME FRAPPUCCINO

Prep Time: 5 Min

Serving: 1

INGREDIENTS:

1 cup (240 milliliters) milk
2 cups ice
1-1/2 tbsp (20 gram) powder sugar.
5 frozen strawberries.
Whipped cream (optional)

INSTRUCTIONS:

Blend milk, ice, powder sugar and frozen strawberry until smooth.
Pour into the glass and top with whipped cream if desired.
Garnish with fresh strawberries.

GREEN TEA FRAPPUCCINO

Prep Time: 5 Min

Serving: 1

INGREDIENTS:

1 cup (240 milliliters) milk
2 cups ice
1 tablespoon matcha green tea powder
2 tablespoons sugar

INSTRUCTIONS:

Combine milk, ice, matcha powder, and sugar in a blender.
Blend until smooth.
Pour into a glass and serve immediately.

PUMPKIN SPICE FRAPPUCCINO

Prep Time: 5 Min

Serving: 1

INGREDIENTS:

1 cup (240 milliliters) cold brewed coffee
2 cups ice
1/4 cup (60 milliliters) pumpkin puree
1 teaspoon pumpkin spice
1/4 cup (60 milliliters) milk
Whipped cream (optional)

INSTRUCTIONS:

Blend coffee, ice, pumpkin puree, spice, and milk until smooth. Pour into the serving glass and top with whipped cream. Sprinkle additional pumpkin spice on top for garnish.

MINT MOCHA FRAPPUCCINO

Prep Time: 5 Min

Serving: 1

INGREDIENTS:

1 cup (240 milliliters) cold brewed coffee
2 cups ice
1/4 cup (60 milliliters) chocolate syrup
1/8 teaspoon mint extract
Whipped cream and chocolate shavings (optional)

INSTRUCTIONS:

Blend coffee, ice, chocolate syrup, and mint extract until smooth.
Pour into a glass and serve immediately.
Optional: top the drink with whipped cream and chocolate shavings for garnish.

SALTED CARAMEL MOCHA FRAPPUCCINO

Prep Time: 5 Min

Serving: 1

INGREDIENTS:

1 cup (240 milliliters) cold brewed coffee
2 cups ice
1/4 cup (60 milliliters) caramel syrup
Pinch of sea salt
Whipped cream and extra caramel syrup (optional)

INSTRUCTIONS:

Blend coffee, ice, caramel syrup, and a pinch of sea salt until smooth.
Pour into the serving glass and top with whipped cream if desired.
Drizzle extra caramel syrup over the top and serve immediately.

RASPBERRY COFFEE MILKSHAKE

Prep Time: 5 Min

Serving: 1

INGREDIENTS:

1 cup (240 milliliters) cold brewed coffee
2 scoops (about 100 grams) of raspberry ice cream
1/2 cup (120 milliliters) milk
1 teaspoon (5 milliliters) vanilla syrup

INSTRUCTIONS:

Combine cold coffee, raspberry ice cream, milk, and vanilla syrup in a blender. Blend until smooth.
Pour into the tall glass and serve immediately. Optionally garnish with fresh raspberries and whipped cream.

COFFEE COCKTAILS

Unite the worlds of caffeine and spirits with our Coffee Cocktails. These sophisticated blends offer a dance of flavors, merging the rich depth of coffee with the allure of alcohol. Dive in and experience the bold fusion of two beloved beverages.

ESPRESSO MARTINI

Prep Time: 5 Min

Serving: 1

INGREDIENTS:

1½ ounces (45 milliliters) vodka
1 ounce (30 millilitres) coffee liqueur (like Kahlua)
1 ounce (30 milliliters) freshly brewed espresso, cooled

INSTRUCTIONS:

Pour vodka, coffee liqueur, and freshly brewed espresso into a cocktail shaker.
Add ice to chill the mixture as it is shaken.
Secure the shaker lid and shake for 15 seconds until chilled.
Pour the mixture into the chilled martini glass.
Optional: garnish with three coffee beans placed in the center of the glass.

IRISH COFFEE

Prep Time: 3 Min

Serving: 1

INGREDIENTS:

1½ ounces (45 milliliters) Irish whiskey
4 ounces (120 milliliters) hot brewed coffee
1 teaspoon (5 grams) brown sugar
Fresh whipped cream

INSTRUCTIONS:

Pre-warm a coffee mug by rinsing it with hot water.
Pour in the Irish whiskey and add the hot coffee until the mug is about three-quarters full.
Dissolve the brown sugar into the coffee-whiskey mix.
Float fresh whipped cream on top by pouring it over the back of a spoon so it rests on the surface of the coffee.

BLACK RUSSIAN

Prep Time: 3 Min

Serving: 1

INGREDIENTS:

2 ounces (60 milliliters) vodka
1 ounce (30 millilitres) coffee liqueur (like Kahlua)

INSTRUCTIONS:

Pour vodka into an old-fashioned glass filled with ice.
Add the coffee liqueur over the vodka.
Stir gently until the mixture is chilled.
Optional: garnish with a cherry.

WHITE RUSSIAN

Prep Time: 3 Min

Serving: 1

INGREDIENTS:

2 ounces (60 milliliters) vodka
1 ounce (30 milliliters) coffee liqueur
1 ounce (30 milliliters) heavy cream or milk

INSTRUCTIONS:

In the serving glass filled with ice, pour the vodka.
Add the coffee liqueur.
Slowly pour the cream or milk over the back of a spoon held over the glass so it floats on top of the liquid.
Stir gently before drinking.

KAHLUA COFFEE

Prep Time: 3 Min

Serving: 1

INGREDIENTS:

1 ounce (30 milliliters) Kahlua
6 ounces (180 milliliters) hot brewed coffee
Whipped cream

INSTRUCTIONS:

Pour the Kahlua into a warm mug.
Add the hot coffee and stir gently to combine.
Top the mug with a generous dollop of whipped cream.
Optional: garnish with a sprinkle of cocoa powder or chocolate shavings.

NUTTY IRISHMAN

Prep Time: 5 Min

Serving: 1

INGREDIENTS:

1 ounce (30 milliliters) Irish cream liqueur
1 ounce (30 millilitres) Frangelico (hazelnut liqueur)
6 ounces (180 milliliters) hot brewed coffee
Whipped cream (optional)

INSTRUCTIONS:

In a warm mug, pour Irish cream and Frangelico.
Add the hot coffee and stir gently to combine.
Top with whipped cream, then sprinkle chopped hazelnuts for garnish if desired.

MEXICAN COFFEE WITH TEQUILA AND KAHLUA

Prep Time: 5 Min

Serving: 1

INGREDIENTS:

1 ounce (30 milliliters) Kahlua
1 ounce (30 milliliters) tequila
6 ounces (180 milliliters) hot brewed coffee
Whipped cream (optional)

INSTRUCTIONS:

Combine Kahlua and tequila in a warm coffee mug.
Pour in the hot coffee and stir gently.
If desired, decorate with whipped cream and a sprinkle of cinnamon.

BOURBON SPIKED HOT COFFEE

Prep Time: 5 Min

Serving: 1

INGREDIENTS:

1½ ounces (45 milliliters) bourbon
6 ounces (180 milliliters) hot brewed coffee
1 teaspoon (5 grams) sugar (adjust to taste)
Whipped cream (optional)

INSTRUCTIONS:

Pour bourbon into a warm mug, then add hot coffee.
Add sugar, stirring until dissolved.
Top with whipped cream if desired.

CAFÉ AMORE WITH AMARETTO AND COGNAC

Prep Time: 5 Min

Serving: 1

INGREDIENTS:

1 ounce (30 milliliters) Amaretto
1 ounce (30 milliliters) Cognac
6 ounces (180 milliliters) hot brewed coffee
Whipped cream and shaved almonds (optional)

INSTRUCTIONS:

In a warm mug, combine Amaretto and Cognac.
Add hot coffee and stir gently.
Garnish with whipped cream and shaved almonds if desired.

SPANISH COFFEE

Prep Time: 5 Min

Serving: 1

INGREDIENTS:

½ oz. (15 milliliters) rum
½ oz. (15 milliliters) Kahlua
½ oz. (15 milliliters) triple sec
6 ounces (180 milliliters) hot brewed coffee
Whipped cream and ground nutmeg (optional)

INSTRUCTIONS:

In a warmed mug, pour rum, Kahlua, and triple sec.
Add hot coffee, stirring gently to combine.
Top with whipped cream and a dash of nutmeg if desired.

COFFEE OLD FASHIONED

Prep Time: 5 Min

Serving: 1

INGREDIENTS:

1½ ounces (45 milliliters) bourbon or rye whiskey
1/2 ounce (15 millilitres) simple syrup
2 dashes of Angostura bitters
1 ounce (30 milliliters) cold brew coffee
Orange twist and cherry for garnish

INSTRUCTIONS:

Combine whiskey, simple syrup, Angostura bitters, and cold-brew coffee in a mixing glass.
Pour ice into the serving glass and stir until well chilled.
Strain into a rock glass filled with large ice cubes.
Decorate with an orange twist and a cherry.

COLD BREW NEGRONI

Prep Time: 5 Min

Serving: 1

INGREDIENTS:

1 ounce (30 milliliters) gin
1 ounce (30 milliliters) Campari
1 ounce (30 milliliters) sweet vermouth
1 ounce (30 milliliters) cold brew coffee
Orange twist for garnish

INSTRUCTIONS:

Combine gin, Campari, sweet vermouth, and cold brew coffee in a mixing glass.
Add ice to the serving glass, chill, and stir until the mixture is well chilled.
Strain into a rock glass over ice.
Garnish with an orange twist.

AMARETTO TIRAMISU COFFEE

Prep Time: 5 Min

Serving: 1

INGREDIENTS:

1 cup (240 milliliters) brewed coffee
1 teaspoon (5 milliliters) vanilla syrup
1 teaspoon (5 milliliters) chocolate sauce
1 tablespoon (15 milliliters) amaretto or almond-flavored liqueur
whipped cream for topping

INSTRUCTIONS:

Pour brewed coffee into a mug. Add Vanilla Syrup, Chocolate Sauce, Amaretto, or almond liqueur to the coffee.
Stir well until all ingredients are combined. Top with whipped cream and serve.

CONCLUSION

Embark on an enchanting journey through "The Ultimate Coffee Recipe Book," where each page turns a delightful new chapter in your coffee experience. From the cozy warmth of classic lattes to the invigorating splash of unique, tantalizing flavors, this book promises a coffee journey that awakens the senses and soothes the soul.

Explore the realm of coffee creativity with 101 meticulously crafted recipes that unfold a rich tapestry of tastes and aromas. Each cup, each sip, brings you a step closer to the exquisite symphony of coffee's captivating allure. Our curated selection guides you through reimagined classics, the allure of infused syrups, and the bold adventure of diverse, global coffee styles.

Dive deep into the heart of coffee's enchanting world with "The Ultimate Coffee Recipe Book." Unlock the secrets to transforming your coffee moments into unforgettable experiences that linger warmly in your memories, making every day more vibrant and meaningful. Let the aroma fill your space, and let the flavors tell their stories—one extraordinary coffee at a time

Made in the USA
Monee, IL
21 December 2024